Ghana: West Africa Mi

D1526051

On A Mission for God

BELINDA MCBROOM

Copyright © 2021 Belinda McBroom.

All Rights Reserved

ISBN-9798453216727

Publishing By The Creative Short Book Writers Project
Wayne Drumheller, Editor and Founder
Printing and Publishing: Platform: KDP.amazon.com.

Disclaimer

The author has made every effort to ensure the accuracy of the information within this book was correct at time of publication. The information provided within this book is for general education and information use only. Acknowledgement of sources has been granted for individual articles or authors for the use of their information on Reference page 96 in this book. The methods and ideas described within this book are based on the author's experiences, and reviews of professionals and expert internet resources in writing, editing and independent publishing. You may discover there are other methods and materials to accomplish the same end result.

Contact Minister Belinda McBroom on the Internet:

www.belindamcbroom.com

Table of Contents

Dedication

Acknowledgements

Preface

Introduction

Ghana: West Africa Mission (1999)

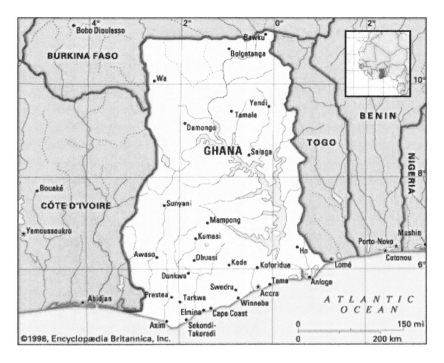

Map of Ghana

DEDICATION AND APPRECIATIONS

First and foremost, I thank God for leading and guiding me to do His will. Without faith and prayer to the Almighty no visions can be accomplished in this earthly life. Because of His Greater love for me, my love for God comes before any and everyone.

ACKNOWLEDGEMENTS

I dedicate this book to my immediate family: husband Gregory; four children: Melissa, Penny, Jeremy, Joshua; two sisters: Ruby and Ryann; late brother Theodore Jr., and most of all to my beautiful granddaughters, Kayla, Elizabeth, and Olivia. I also devote these writings to my late parents Theodore Roosevelt Foust, Sr., and Agnes Alston Foust and to my late mother-in-law Hattie McBroom Clough. My heart and soul love all the aforementioned. They sacrificed time and love during my ministry and missionary ventures. Thank you to my friends Sharon Braswell, Patricia Marion, Elder Gloria Sutton, my personal mentor; Linda Bonner, M.Ed., and Affini Woodley for their contribution and support of this project. I acknowledge my fellow church members, neighbors, and anyone who prayed for the African missionary team.

Thanks to Dr. Joseph Rogers, Sr. for his prayers, suggestions and help through the process of this book.

PREFACE

I wrote this book in memory of the late Bishop Leonard "Foday" Farrar who passed in 2015, about fifteen years after the trip, which was in August 1999. He was a very humble man of God who led all the national churches who joined the Foreign Mission of the Full Gospel Baptist Church Fellowship International. A pastor who heard from God, he was loved and admired very much around the world. Bishop Farrar preached and taught the Word of God in and out of season! He was truly a man that was full of the spirit of God, one that put thinking into action.

I can remember it was the year of twenty fourteen that I called and talked to Bishop Farrar. I asked to write this "book" on his behalf and on the behalf of the country of Ghana, West Africa. He was so enthused that I would even ask that question. That is just the way he was, one that showed joy in the Lord and what life had to offer him. I talked various times to him that year about the book. The Full Gospel Church "planted" churches in various parts of the African continent. I wondered, "Was this a Mission from God and was Pastor Leonard "Foday" Farrar commissioned by the Lord to go to Ghana, West Africa?" That is just one question that I had on my mind to ask him!

Well, Wednesday, January twenty-eight, twenty-fifteen, I had my chance to do a phone interview that afternoon with Pastor Farrar. He had preached earlier that morning about the name that the African men had given him. So, I asked him about it. I said, "What does your middle name mean?" He stated that his African brother said "Foday" meant "Very Holy man." And when he got back into the United States, one year after his journey to Sierra Leone, he immediately changed his name on his birth certificate. His middle name was now officially "Foday." He also told me how the task of the "Mission Journey" got started. While leasing the church on Holman Drive, Garner, NC five years before the Ghana trip, the Church decided to have a "Perspective on Mission."

They invited different speakers each night. Reverend Elgin Taylor was one of the speakers who flew to

North Carolina. Pastor Farrar picked him up from the airport. He said, "It was the first time I ever met this man." Reverend Taylor stayed with one of the New Canaan members and her husband. Pastor said shortly after that, the two of them started making plans for church members desiring to pay for the mission trip to Ghana, West Africa.

Reverend Taylor knew the area, people in many parts of Africa. After their meeting, Pastor Farrar wanted to take a trip to Africa, and the planning took six years and ensued in August of 1999.

There were two different areas our team, led by Reverend Taylor and Pastor Farrar visited while in Africa. One was Accra and the other was Kumasi. These two neighboring places were fascinating to visit in western area of Africa. An African tour guide drove us there in an old, blue, and white bus that held twenty passengers and their luggage. The men worked on it a couple of times to restart for the five hour and two-minute drive.

Accra is the capital of Ghana, on the Atlantic coast of West Africa. Accra is the administrative, economic, and educational center of Ghana. The city contained the head offices of all the large banks and trading firms, insurance agencies, electrical corporations, a general post office and large open markets from which most of the food supply comes, and the Accra Central Library. Accra has well paved roads and an efficient municipal bus service. It also features a transportation hub. The city is connected by rail to Kumasi.

Kumasi is the capital city of the Ashanti region in southern Ghana. This city's traditions such as funeral arrangements, family life, and textile making became the focus of attention. There was a broad variety of attractions in this city. In the northern part of the town, was the headquarters of the Ashanti king and representatives in his twenty-room royal household with three or more wings. In the northern part of this area was the Manhyia Palace.

There is a courtroom and courtyard in this Manhyia Palace where issues dealing with traditions and statutes are considered by the customary committee. Tourists and guests can get a good awareness of customary African democratic systems. When the people in Kumasi visit the courtyard, the customs are very current to them.

Southeast of Kumasi is Lake Bosumtwi. It is about 32 kilometers and is the largest lake in Ghana. One belief the Ashanti have is that farewell is made to a God called Twi. When their souls die, it comes to the lake. An idea or notion is that the lake was formed by a meteorite. One more thing that is said about the lake is that it represents a pit of a nonexistent volcano. I want you to know that this book is not just about Missions, but about the experiences I have had with the people of Ghana and its culture.

INTRODUCTION

My never-ending faith in God has led me to finally complete this book describing my trip to Ghana, West Africa, a gloriously personal experience. It is my hope that this book will inspire other Americans to take the journey to Africa, our homeland, to reconnect with our heritage and ancestry dating back to the seventeenth century.

My personal journey to get to Ghana started one Sunday morning when our Pastor, Bishop L. Foday Farrar, of Solid Rock Ministry International, Garner, NC talked to the congregation about the need to staff the Prayer Room with members committing to one hour of prayer.

God lifted my spirit to respond to the divine request from Bishop Farrar. In the same week of his appeal, I signed up to pray in the Prayer Room on Saturdays from four to five in the afternoon, a profoundly serious and heartfelt undertaking. In answering the call to serve in the Prayer Room, I also answered the call by God to be an Intercessor for those who needed thoughtful, fervent, and consistent warfare prayers. I began to spend time reading letters from missionary leaders from third world countries which led to increased empathy for the impoverished natives.

Bishop Farrar began to minister powerfully through his sermons about foreign missions, with each message penetrating the hearts of those desiring to commit to the journey. After praying incessantly and presenting my petition to the Lord, I said, "Yes, I will go!" to Bishop Farrar. The Lord spoke even stronger in our hearts to form missionaries. A committed church family, both young and old, interceded.

An intense sense of heartfelt love for the Lord, Church, Pastor, and the African people overcame us. Pastor had taught us well about submissiveness to God's will. As the Lord continued to speak through him, church teams started to apply for our passports as we prepared to travel to the wealthy, yet spiritually depleted continent of Africa.

We gave ourselves time to prepare to do the will of the Lord. He had spoken to our hearts to go; and that is what the newly formed missionaries prepared for. As the process of applying for passports started and departure drew closer, we experienced a lot of highs and lows as we pressed to do the will of the Lord. This is my testimony of this powerful and life changing experience.

Luke 14:23 was the scripture that assisted many to an excellent lead-in for the missionary field: "*And the lord said unto the servant, go out into the highways and hedges, and compel them to come in, that my house may be filled."*

(1) Master Study Bible

Missionaries are: *"Christians called to do the will of the Lord."* They are to pray for the souls of others in need. Praying for all people, people in Africa and those in third world countries. People of all ethnic groups need prayer, there are no exceptions. Believers attempt missionary work arduously. They travel to preach and teach the Word of God to every human being (Mark 16:15).

PRAYER

Prayer is defined as an act of petitioning, praising, giving thanks, or confessing to God; it is expressed by several different words in both the Old Testament and the New Testaments. (Harper Collins' Bible Dictionary). A prayer room is a "secret closet" or a place where people go to offer up prayers to the Lord our God. It is a place of privacy and isolation between spiritual humans and the Lord. It is a spot of peace, where individuals send prayers to the Almighty Savior who hears all.

Man has direct access to God through prayer. When he prays, it gives Him legal rights and permission to intervene in any earthly matter. God faithfully answers prayers. (Dr. Myles Munroe *Understanding the Purpose and Power of Prayer*)

Chapter One

Preparing for Ghana

In 1996, divine intercession began as events unfolded in my life as I struggled to make plans to fly to Africa. As a prayer warrior, an intercessor, I was able to pray for strength, guidance and wisdom as earthly matters prevented a smooth path forward. An intercessor is one that communes with God as He reveals situations and circumstances to use an individual to intercede or pray on behalf of another.

As I started making the plans for the trip to Africa, opposition began to arise. It kept coming in my daily life like a severe thunderstorm! Everything was turned up-side down, right up until the day I departed. I told my cousin about my travel plans to Africa and how the Lord wanted to use me on this mission. He was upset, not understanding the call of God for my assignment, and told me that the Lord did not tell me to go! He insisted that all I needed was some rest.

He told me that he would keep my children while my husband, Gregory, and I planned a mini vacation. The argument was very heated and intense, but I knew in my heart what the Lord was saying to me, and I was determined to do His will.

A few days after the discussion with my cousin, while working in the jewelry department at Wal-Mart, I returned from my break and there was a message for me to call home. When I called home, my husband said someone had called from the University of North Carolina Memorial

Hospital, Chapel Hill NC and he said, "If you want to see your mother, hurry up and get here!" I left work immediately to drive the distance of thirty-one miles to the hospital.

Not knowing what to expect, I prayed for God to intervene on behalf of my mother. I wrestled with thoughts of what I could have done to prevent this sudden grave illness. The thirty-one-mile drive seemed more like one hundred. The yellow lines in the highway started merging as one huge yellow road, but by the grace and mercy of God, I made it to the hospital without incident.

Once at the hospital, my path was directly to the Emergency Room. The first family members that I saw were my aunts, who told me that my mother needed brain surgery and her condition was critical. The doctors would know something after the surgery. The surgery was a success, thank God!

A few days later, the doctors told us that a second surgery was needed. I remember going to the chapel in the hospital and crying out to the Lord; praying that He would bring her through this second surgery, and He did. I was so thankful to the Lord! After a few weeks at the hospital in Chapel Hill, my mother was transferred to the Vancor Rehabilitation Center in Greensboro, NC to be weaned off the ventilator. After her release from the rehabilitation center, and to be able to take care of my mother, I had to transfer to the Wal-Mart location in Burlington, NC. The job transfer was not the only area of impact, I also had to change schools for three of my four children.

We would spend the week at my mother's house and commute back home to my husband for the weekends.

About three weeks later, I started working with a company in Burlington doing personal care for clients. This experience as a personal care assistant helped qualify me to care for my mother as the primary live-in caregiver. As a devoted family, we loved Mom and worked together to tend and care for all her daily needs, nothing concerning her immediate care was left undone by her family! With the many changes within the family, the children started getting adjusted to school in the new area. During this time, I was still trying to get things prepared for the trip to Africa. The children, my husband, and all my family members, knew of my plans to go to Africa.

The week before leaving for Africa I had a serious talk with the children about thoughts and prayers of them while being out of the United States. We all acknowledged our goodbyes that day. The plan was for our three children to stay home in Raleigh with their dad. My youngest son would stay with his father's mother through the week, and his father would pick him up on the weekends.

My mother's home health nurse came and checked on my mother for her medical needs once a week. During the last week I told her of my plans of being out of the country. She had a strange expression on her face as I told her what the Lord had placed on my heart to do. She told me she knew I was not going at a time like this, when my mother was still extremely sick. I told her I had to go, that the Lord had put this on my heart and that I had no choice, but to obey Him, I had to go! Though she questioned my going on the trip, our conversation ended on an incredibly positive note.

Finalizing Plans

The coordinator of Foreign Mission at New Canaan Full Gospel Baptist Church in Garner, North Carolina, assisted me in preparation for the long journey to Africa. During the preparation time, I wrote letters asking people to help fund my mission trip to Ghana, West Africa. I reminded the people of the mandate from Jesus Christ concerning the Great Commission. The Mandate was given to the disciples of Jesus Christ to:

"Go ye therefore, and teach all nations, baptizing them in the name of the Father, and of the Son, and of the Holy Ghost: Teaching them to observe all things whatsoever I have commanded you: and, lo, I am with you always, even unto the end of the world. Amen." (Matthew 28:19-20)

The preparation process required me to take shots, have the immunization records, and attend a training class for the mission trip to Africa.

Getting shots consisted of three visits to the doctor and taking malaria pills for ten days before departure and this required me to travel some twenty-eight point seven miles to the Health Clinic in Greensboro, NC.

Passports are required when visiting outside of the United States, the process is extensive, yet necessary for international travel.

The Training Class introduced us to the customs and laws of Africa, and the strategically planned activities while on the trip.

The assistant pastor at Solid Rock taught the training class on what we, as Missionaries, should expect during our journey to the foreign land. He prepared our minds and hearts on how to act and react to the things that would and could happen on the trip.

The most challenging opposition was the delay of my passport prior to the departure date of the mission trip. The coordinator informed me that all funding for the mission trip did not meet the deadline date. After several telephone calls, many problems with the passport delay and lack of funds were resolved. I was thrilled that the Lord had touched hearts to sponsor me as a missionary.

On August 8, 1999, the trip was made possible. It was Sunday, a good day for travel. That day we met at Raleigh/Durham Airport about 10:00 am. During this year it was around the time of the Second Civil War in Liberia. My husband drove me to the Raleigh-Durham International Airport, where we met others on our team that were going to Ghana, West Africa. It would be a trip of a lifetime for me. As we rode to the airport, I told my husband various things to do concerning the children. At the time, he was a truck driver. We again reviewed the plans for how the children would be cared for and where they would stay. Melissa, Penny and Jeremy would stay at home and baby Joshua would be at my husband's mother's house.

I could never imagine traveling to another country. I remember taking a class at Shaw University and telling some of my classmates about my plan of going overseas and how excited they were for me. As I spoke about Ghana West Africa, one of my classmates said, "You are going to the motherland." I listened to her as she made that statement. Those words touched something within my heart. Little did I know the deep connection we as African Americans really had with Africa and the African people. This was my first trip, and I did not know what to expect.

All I knew was that this was a time of praying and

interceding for those in another country and to listen to God

as he spoke to me through prayer and fasting. Giving

praise to the Lord for all he was doing in my life for my

family, that I love very much. Now I had to leave my

husband, the girls, son, and baby Joshua, but I knew I had

to go. God had spoken to me to be a missionary, an

ambassador for the Lord Jesus Christ. As it was now time to get ready to make the most important step of my life, to go and board that plane not knowing what to really expect, I had to do it! "There is no turning back now" I thought to myself. God had given me the assurance that everything would be alright with my family, the children, and my husband.

Raleigh-Durham Airport

American Missionary at RDU

Raleigh-Durham United Airport is in Morrisville, NC. This is where our missionary team met to begin our flight to Ghana, West Africa. Upon our arrival, the people there had a great expression of joy and excitement, but also calmness was expressed on the faces of some of our mission team.

My husband and I went to talk with Pastor Farrar and his wife and others going on the trip. We greeted them and engaged in general conversation about how everything was going. Talking a little bit about the ride to the airport. Then, there was talk about our tickets, the flight, and things we need to do at the airport. After that everyone talked among themselves.

Saying good-bye to my husband and letting him know I love him. Telling him to take care of the children. He agreed and said he would. He left and started back home.

About twenty minutes later a voice came over the loudspeaker announcing our flight to Charlotte Airport, NC. We boarded the flight with our carry-on luggage in our hand, and I also had my white feather sleeping pillow in my arm.

Charlotte Airport

After flying from Raleigh-Durham Airport, we landed at Charlotte Airport in NC. This flight took about thirty minutes. Our group met other Missionaries that joined our group to travel to Ghana West Africa. This was a great fellowship of meeting people from another state, Maryland. Pastor John Jenkins, two of his Ministers, one guy that resided in Maryland but was originally from West Africa and others were met in Charlotte from Gleneden First Baptist (MD). I had visited Washington, DC, and Maryland sometime while growing up because my oldest sister, her husband and son stayed there. I used to babysit their son in the nineteen seventies when out of school for the summer. So, I knew a little bit about the area where they lived.

London Airport

When we arrived in London, Bishop Farrar and the team met with Reverend Elgin Taylor, International Director of Christians in Action. Reverend Taylor would be joining our team along with his wife and two others traveling to Ghana. The Taylors lived in London. They had several children, one son that also lived in London. The Taylors were exceptionally good people, lively and full of zeal. Reverend Taylor and his wife carried conversations that would get anybody's attention as they talked with them. There was excitement that filled the airport as we listened to Sister Dorothy Taylor talk about London and the queen. Another elderly female also joined us as a part of the missionary journey. Becoming acquainted with everyone in the group, we found out we had a 5-hour layover in the

London Airport. The layover caught everyone in our group by surprise.

We thought we would fly straight through instead of having a five-hour layover in any part of our flight. After the depressing news of the layover, our team got busy trying to occupy the time with things to do in the airport. Now we had more time to fellowship, carry on conversations with one another, and laugh! It was more of a spirit of joy in the atmosphere. Everyone relaxed and just accepted the time we had to wait for our next flight. Some of our team read books, The Bible, or magazines. Some used their cellphone to call home. We all went to the food court upstairs to get our lunch.

There were several vendors that sold all different kinds of food. After lunch that evening, some in our group were tempted to go out on the streets of London to sightsee. However, we were warned by Reverend Taylor's wife. She said that we did not want to take that chance of getting lost and end up missing our flight to Accra, Ghana. As we listened, we all agreed to what she was saying and stayed in the airport. After we stayed in the airport for several hours, our time was approaching for the next flight. We got our hand-held things together and listened for our boarding information.

Our team boarded the plane departing from London/Gatwick. Our team was aboard the "The Boeing 777." This aircraft is unique. It has a superb variety of customer-ideal comfort and creates long-range success for carriers around the world. Comforts such as the seats. The seats were reclinable and well cushioned. The temperature setting was perfect, and the flow of air was not

overwhelming. Also, this plane has superior fuel efficiency.

This was an excellent plane to fly the long distance across

the Atlantic Ocean. It was a peaceful ride that welcomed

passengers to sleep.

Chapter Two

Flying Through the Storm

While the plane flew over the Atlantic Ocean, some challenges occurred. It was very frightening. I remember it being dark as I awoke from sleep. The plane was in flight and sudden anxiety came upon me.

We were in the middle of a thunderstorm, and it was raining awfully hard. The weather was rough and as I looked outside my window; I could see lightning. The plane hit air pockets and turbulence in mid-air. All sorts of negative thoughts filled my mind.

I had ridden on a plane before, but I must say, never this far!

I have flown from Florida to North Carolina and from Washington D.C. to the south, but this flight was different. The thoughts that plagued my mind were feelings about the pilot and being in mid-air. Then I started to pray, continually letting the Lord know I was completely and totally in His Holy hands, through it all saying the Lord was flying the plane.

My prayer

Father God I pray in the name of Jesus Lord that You protect everyone on this plane. Lord that you keep us safe. God, I pray that you guide the pilot. Lord, I pray that you take control of the steering wheel and drive this plane! Thank you, Jesus!

The solution I gathered from this incident is that the key to any problem is prayer. In moments of discouragement, trials, and fears or when a person feels so alone like nobody cares and turns it over to Jesus. He will make everything alright. Just a little talk with Jesus will make everything alright. The storm lasted most of the night and I stayed awake throughout the duration of the trip from London to Accra, Ghana.

It was still dark as the plane landed in Accra, in a field! I was in shock, it was completely dark, there were only huge spotlights around the area, but there was no airport! I could not believe it. The pilot had landed in a field with no buildings around, but there were a lot of African men, young and old. Distress started to grip my mind all over again and again I started praying. It was pitch black dark! No other light in sight! There were African men all around us. I thought about the Bible scripture 2 Tim. 1:7, *"For God has not given us the spirit of fear, but of power, and of love, and of a sound mind."*

Evidently these African men were taxi drivers. They talked to our American men and the African man from the Ivory Coast who had traveled with us from Maryland. Thank God the men traveling with our missionary team handled the situation. They talked to the men and let them know we did not need transportation but were waiting for our guide. It was about ten to fifteen minutes when our bus driver drove up. I started to feel at ease when I saw our driver arrive on the bus. There was a sigh of relief that came upon me, and I am sure upon others in our American group.

After our guide had arrived at the Airport in Ghana the men from the USA put our luggage on the bus. Our first stop was a couple's house in this city, it was daybreak.

Everyone was tired and exhausted from the trip. We were first taken to the couple's house to rest and relax from the journey. They were very hospitable and welcoming. The couple opened their home, gave us a place to rest and refresh. We rested there for a few hours. Our group helped prepare breakfast and ate before we left.

An altercation started because of breakfast duties within our missionary group. There was a conversation before leaving the USA that while being on the trip problems would arise, and that is exactly what happened. But thanks to God, the difficulties were resolved right then and there.

It was so great to be around Christian friends! We were able to fellowship, socialize and know we had one plan. That plan was to do the will of the Lord Jesus Christ, oh that was such a joy! That day within the couples' House there was a sense of peace and calmness that filled the atmosphere around us. We were there to join in one common goal for the Father on High and that was to do whatever He was commanding us to do. It was a sensational and joyful time for the whole Missionary team.

Travel to Accra

At about one o'clock we proceeded on to the destination Accra. The ride was very peaceful and relaxing. As we arrived and went into "The Pink Panther Motel." This motel was genuinely nice and had various sections, the one-story wood building while the restaurant had a glass front.

Across the street was a lumberyard or possibly a wood making company, I was not certain of its actual business nature. Once we got to our motel, we attempted to check in, only to discover that my roommate and I did not have a room.

We had the reservation, but there was a mix up. Two guys from our group also had a problem with their room. So, the front desk staff decided to give us rooms in the guest house.

It was perfect. We not only had one, but two rooms with a kitchen and a big lounging area. After all the luggage was put in our rooms, we freshened up and then met back in the motel dining area. We ate a good meal and once again fellowshipped.

After we came out of the motel restaurant there were merchants outside, waiting for our group. The people had all kinds of African attire set up for our group to look at and see. There were complete outfits, dresses, all kinds of apparel and jewelry. We examined the clothing and a variety of other merchandise, and some members of our group bought items that evening.

I bought a black and white tribal necklace and bracelet. I also purchased a green African outfit and a gold African dress. After buying these items, I realized one of the ladies from our team was financially unable to purchase an outfit. I thought to myself I have these two different types of clothing and an outfit from the United States. After talking to her about the dress and extra skirt sets I had, she agreed with me that she would accept the green outfit. I was thankful she decided to receive the outfit. She was happy and I was overjoyed that she had accepted my gift. I also thought "Why not bless someone else on the trip?" Everybody seems to want to look out for everyone else's needs. Our group wanted to make sure no one lacked for anything which caused everyone to be happy and excited to be on the trip.

The skirt outfit I had bought in the United States was from a salesperson in Garner, NC. This foreigner who owned a little shop on main street sold all African clothing. She would travel back and forth to New York where she purchased clothing and brought them back to Garner and sold them in her clothing store. I would go by her shop somedays and look at the fabulous attire, pocketbooks, and jewelry she would show me. I brought a few pieces of items from her shop.

While looking and buying clothing in Accra that evening, I met a thirteen-year-old boy, he was a very bright young man of African descent. This young man was there with the merchants outside our motel where he greeted our missionary group. He reminded me of my sons back in America. He had questions about salvation and the Christian life. He was trying to make the decision about being saved. As it was late in the evening, I talked to him a little bit about becoming a Christian.

Minister McBroom at Guesthouse at Motel in Ghana

Later, that week my roommate and I invited the
young boy into the guest house. Some of our American
men and women discussed the plan of Salvation with the
young Ghanaian man. We also let him know if he turned
from his wicked ways and confessed with his mouth, the
"Lord Jesus, he would be saved. The scripture from the
Holy Bible, Romans 10:9-10 was quoted to him:

9 That if thou shalt confess with thy mouth the Lord Jesus, and shalt believe in thine heart that God hath raised him from the dead, thou shalt be saved. 10 For with the heart man believeth unto righteousness; and with the mouth confession is made unto salvation.

Apostle Paul wrote to the Corinthian church, *"I have planted, Apollos watered; but God gave the increase."* (1 Corinth. 3:6)

Paul was talking about the Plan of Salvation. He planted the seed of the Gospel of Christ and Apollos watered the seed, but ultimately God gave the increase. Paul and Apollos were Holy men of God. They were Gods' representatives. They were equipped to speak to individuals about being saved. As believers we can let an unsaved person know God's plan for salvation and another person can also confirm God's plan, but only God can work on the heart of the individual for them to accept Jesus Christ as their "personal savior."

I prayed we had planted a seed in his heart, to one day accept Jesus Christ as his personal savior. We know the Bible says one planted, one water, but God brings the increase. So, I know we did what the Lord had asked us. After our counseling, he was thankful for the information and advice that we had shared with him. Others in our missionary team talked to him about salvation and the Christian way as he listened with intensive ears.

During the time we were over in Africa there was war going on. The Second Liberian Civil War began in 1999 and ended in October 2003 in the attempt by the UN and US military forces to stop the rebel siege on Monrovia. Charles Taylor was exiled to Nigeria until he was arrested in 2006 and taken to The Hague for his trial. The conclusion of this war left two hundred fifty thousand people killed and nearly one million displaced. During this time, our Pastor and First Lady were not at the motel. They had boarded a private flight to Sierra Leone, Africa. Some team members said they were to explore an area that had been bombed. Our missionary group came together and started praying about the trip and their safe return. That day we stayed at the motel and visited with one another.

Talking about ourselves and things in the United States such as our family, church, and jobs. We used our time wisely with fellowship. We talked about Africa and the area we were in. We were astonished how more advanced everything was like the clothing and the fact they had running water. We also marveled at the streets because they were exceptionally clean and tidy.

That evening our Pastor and First Lady finally returned. We rejoiced and welcomed them back to our group. We were able to rest and were at peace that God answered our prayers for their safe return. We believed that God had worked a miracle to bring them safely back to us.

Chapter Three

Visiting the African Chief

One day our group went to visit one of the Chiefs in his estate. The bus ride was not far from our Motel. I do not remember if our Pastor or Rev. Taylor told us of the visit. They might have told us when the bus had arrived at the Chief's abode. We were escorted on the side of the Chief's building by his council. We were incredibly quiet and did not make any type of noise as we walked through this area. His palace had several establishments connected to it. When our group walked through the development, we were in a large area with several porches. The foundation of the house was in a large square. Some of our group sat in that square on chairs, while some stood up and others sat on the porches.

The chief came out and sat down near the men from our group and with the aid of a translator they talked back and forth. The women in our group did not open their mouths to speak during this exchange among the men. We sat in silence as the men talked. One must think being a woman in another country, "Doesn't a female have the right to speak?" There are certain customs and laws in African culture that one must respect. After about thirty minutes of talking, we said our goodbyes and left the area.

As our missionary group traveled on the road that same day, we saw a funeral procession taking place. There were large groups of people who walked along the road. They were all dressed in African attire. The celebration would consist of a month of festivities in remembrance of the deceased's life before and after death.

There was a lady who was a Minister. She joined our group a few days after we arrived in Africa. She said, "I come every year to this African area to help the Ghanaians to start businesses and trading." However, she also added every time there was a funeral their business would fail because they would take off a month for the funerals. As their company was closed for a month, they would lose customers and the business would fail.

Funerals in Africa are traditional and have certain customs. They take the death of a loved one very seriously. Ghana, West African funerals are usually on Saturdays though some villages have funerals on other days of the week. The customary colors are "black" or "black and red."

The funeral and time of mourning can last one to four weeks, sometime longer.

We visited the Subriso Ghana village where the people were having a church service. This place was surrounded by a few houses and trees in the area. Of course, we joined in and enjoyed the choir and the people. That day the African women danced with power and strength as if to get a breakthrough. As we joined in the celebration, I knew these were our people.

Reverend Elgin Taylor indicated that Subriso was one of the less affluent villages, but their faces really beamed with joy as they danced and worshiped the Lord. They plan to build a more permanent church building. Ghana, Techiman was the best part of our visit where there was a dedication of the new church building. We gave financially to help with the building of this church in this

village. This was the Subriso Ghana village church that involved dancing by church mothers.

The American men and my pastor joined in with the African men as they danced to the music and glorified God. There was joy and excitement everywhere. It seemed to be a dance of victory! These were our African ancestors who had been far in the distance at one point, but now we, their family, African Americans were here in person. We now dance with our culture: those that had been separated from each other now looked each other in the eye and were face to face.

We laughed and had joy. Oh yes, it was a joyous occasion to see my people. People in a foreign land that we connected with well. Our real and spiritual ancestral sisters and brothers in Christ Jesus. That was a day of laughter and joy with our Ghanaian family.

After engaging with the Ghanaians with dancing and singing, the word of God was preached by Pastor Farrar. His message was very uplifting and spoken with power. As many listened with an attentive ear, we were all eager to hear the Lord's message that was given to this man of God. As our group traveled back from the outing that evening, we stopped at a convenience store.

Outside, there was a man asking for money and some people in the group gave him their spare change as they entered the store. Once everyone had returned to the blue and white painted bus and our travels began, someone brought up the fact that in some parts of Africa, the laws are extremely strict. The punishment for thieves would be to have one of their hands amputated and for a woman who was caught committing the act of adultery, her punishment would be a public stoning. Similar lawful consequences could be found in the scripture of the Bible.

Thank God for the teachings of Jesus Christ who told the accusers of the woman caught in adultery, he who is without sin, cast the first stone.

"Jesus had raised Himself up and saw no one but the woman, He said to her, "Woman, where are those accusers of yours? Has no one condemned you?" 11 She said, "No one, Lord." And Jesus said to her, "Neither do I condemn you; go and sin no more." (John 8:10-11)

Our group visited the restaurants while in Ghana. The moment we arrived at the restaurants we saw Iguanas.

They were the only animals we saw in Ghana, West Africa. The iguanas are huge reptiles that stood up on its hind legs like a human. The place these species were mostly seen at were the outsides of the restaurants.

They were in groups of six or seven. It appears the aroma of Ghana's food had drawn them to those locations. With such a large group of reptiles watching us as they searched for food, I immediately talked with the bus driver about my concerns. Once everyone got off the bus, the bus driver would help me to the restaurant.

An African Pastor met with our group and was our host while we visited Ghana. Our group met him at the Royal Basin Restaurant, and he treated us to a meal. He was genuinely nice and shared with us things about the restaurant and the various dishes to eat. He ordered foods that he thought we would like, warning us about the spiciness of certain dishes that may be hotter than we are used to in America. We all engaged in conversation as we ate dinner. As our bodies were only accustomed to American dishes, we took heed to the pastor's words and ate with caution. Some of the Ghanaian dishes were very good. Other foods we tasted did not agree with our taste buds. Overall, I enjoyed the experience and the restaurant had good service.

Thinking about it now, we probably had some of the West African dishes listed within the Flavors of Africa book by Evi Aki. Dishes such as Grilled Tilapia with Ginger Pepper, Yassa (Senegalese Lemon Chicken), Fufu (a pounded yam), Banku (Southern mix of fermented corn and cassava dough, and ridiculously hot pepper, diced tomatoes, and onions) and Jollof Rice just to name a few.

That evening as our group retired to our rooms, my roommate and I had a conversation about the Iguanas and our experiences with other reptiles, insects, and other animals in the USA.

I told her my story about an encounter with one Iguana when my husband and I had first moved to the Wake County area. My husband and I had a paper route, one evening I went to collect from one of the customers. The client invited me into her apartment, and we started talking and I happened to look back and there it was, an Iguana. It was huge, and I was frightened by its appearance. I told the lady if she could just get me to the front door, I would appreciate it. She got between me, and that Iguana animal and we shuffled until I reached the front door. I told her goodbye with a sigh of relief. I was thankful to be out of there. Iguanas are not my favorite animals.

My roommate talked about an experience in her house and the water damage from burst pipes. She told me that she did not know how she was going to get her house fixed; her house was ruined in America with animals living there. One of those animals was a reptile, lizard. She said her mother had gotten sick, so she went to another county to help take care of her. She was living upstairs in her house before she came to Ghana, Africa. So, I encouraged her as she talked.

There was a night she had seen an Iguana in the room, "I was fast asleep in my bed." As she laid awake this reptile appeared out of nowhere. Right then, she said she was going to conquer her fear and she just watched the Iguana that night. She did not tell me anything about the incident until we were sitting on the bus, leaving town.

Two evenings before that we had seen a baby lizard in the top of our closet. My roommate had shared with our pastor and his wife about her experience with an Iguana in our room. They told her not to tell me, because all of them knew I was terrified of those dreadful animals.

That was not the only thing that we talked about our families and other things while in Africa. We talked about the places and things that we had visited in Accra and Kumasi. We talked about the first house we visited after leaving the airport and the great hospitality, generosity the couple gave when our group arrived in Africa.

We read our Bibles several nights and days while in Africa. Every morning I would wake up, go to the bathroom, and pray before we would meet the team and get the day started for travel. I was dedicated to going in the restroom and praying, singing, praising, extolling, and talking to the Lord about my family back home in the United States. I prayed about being in Ghana and the surrounding areas and the other missionaries on the trip, that God would guide us through our time of travel and continue to be with us during the day and throughout the weeks. The spirit of my Savior let me know everything would be alright. I would sense a feeling of peace upon me doing those precious times I spent with God the Father. O it was a "Glorious time to be in the "mother land." This admiration of the Lord brought joy to my heart. It was personal time that I spent with God. Doing this was a part of my prayer life. It helped to make the days go better.

Back at the motel, we had running water. However, when we traveled downtown to get our money exchanged from American to Ghanaian currency, we noticed that alongside the many buildings and cars there was wastewater that flowed beside the street in an open drainage system. The drainage system looked like stone trenches or troughs along either side of the road. The sewage came from the housing and business structures with piping to toilets and sinks. My roommate and I talked about the condition and state of the sewage system as we continued downtown.

While downtown, some of our group took pictures of the buildings, the people, and the vehicles. The streets were clean and free of litter. I did not see anyone outside smoking and the Ghanaian people were quiet.

Economy sized vehicles seemed to be popular to the Ghanaian people as that was the type of car mostly driven. The air was very fresh and appeared to have no pollutants. Wildlife and green trees were scarce in some places. I think we were in the drought season during our visit, though it did rain some days while in West Africa.

As we entered through the door of the white stoned Forex Money Exchange building, a male clerk stood on the other side of the wall, a counter with a glass window with a little metal square opening. Our bus driver told him about our need to exchange our American money to the Ghanaian currency to use while in West Africa. In 1999, 1 US dollar was between 2350 to 3550 Ghana cedis. We visited the

Anyinan Market which housed a variety of vendors including fruits and vegetables. It was strange! It seemed like the people that sold apparel and jewelry outside our motel were also at the marketplace. Maybe they knew we would be there.

The thirteen-year-old young man we had witnessed to at our motel was at the market. Two women were with him. One of these ladies was pregnant. When we saw them, we greeted them, and they did likewise to our team.

Our group continued to look at the food items in the market. Some people bought some of the produce and other items such as sewing cloth, bandannas, crafts, outfits, dresses, skirts, postcards, and maps.

These are the streets of Accra, Africa

The plan for the week was for the women to continue to go to the marketplace while the men went to the Ghana Baptist Seminary to have classes with the young pastors. We were supposed to go back the following week.

However, on that weekend, we were warned that another group was at the marketplace and advised it was best for us not to go as they had different attitudes towards Christians.

It rained that week. A hard rain with some gusts of wind. So, we stayed in the motel. All the women gathered in one room, fellowshipping, and connecting. I remember us talking about the states we were from; one was from New Jersey and another New York. We asked questions like: "Do you have any children? Do you like the area you are living in? What church are you from? And What do you do in ministry?"

After getting to know one another, we began to visit each other's rooms to fellowship and talk further about our experiences while on the mission trip in Ghana. I was able to get to know more about the woman who came every year to help the Ghanaians with their business, Mary was her name.

Supermarket Shopping

On the little blue and white bus, we proceeded to the supermarket. Things we saw while traveling were different businesses and fuel stations. This supermarket would have been called the grocery store back in the United States as our stores would have been a lot bigger. As we entered the store, we compared various things in the supermarket to our grocery stores in America.

There were differences in name brands and a limited selection of items to choose from. We tried to buy things that we were familiar with, not an easy task, yet we did our best. As we proceeded to check out, we used our new Ghanaian money we had exchanged downtown that was African money. The bus driver and an African man from

Maryland that was traveling with us, helped to figure the cost of what we owed at the checkout counter. We were excited when we got on the bus as we discussed the supermarket and the things we had bought for dinner.

Chapter Four

Cape Coast Castle and Ghana's Slave Castles

Visitation to the Cape Coast Castle was a very unusual experience. The Cape Coast Castle was a fortress, it had various rooms and plastered walls. The guide discussed the story of the Ghana Slave Trade about the fortresses and all that took place during the 1400 and through years and centuries of burdensome and hardship of suffering and death to the African people.

People look at the coast of Ghana, and they will find myriad ancient fortresses and castles. Observing the start of the slaves' hazardous journey during the period of the slave trade, these castles were the last remembrance slaves had of their native country before being dispatched throughout the Atlantic, in no way to come back ever again.

During the years of 1482 and 1786, masses of castles and forts were constructed near the 500-kilometer-long seashore of Ghana among Keta in the East and Beyin in the west. Before then Ghana was called the Gold Coast because of its massive quantities of gold, and these fortresses served as strengthened trading posts extending protection from other alien settlers and warnings from the African population.

The Portuguese were positioned intentionally as associations in the trade routes in the 15th century, they were the first colonizers on the Gold Coast, the castles subsequently were detained, condemned, replaced, sold and unrestrained during almost four centuries of fighting between European authorities for control of the Gold Coast.

After seizing gold, ivory and additional wares, the castles progressively incarcerated slaves, who were diminished to yet another article of trade. The magnificent castles along Ghana's splendid coast sheltered mysterious dungeons, bursting with agony and hopelessness, right up until the slave trade was steadily eliminated by each of the colonial forces in the first half of the 1800s. However, by this time, the irrevocable and enormous damage was done, and from West Africa only it is anticipated that six million slaves had been transported to other nations. Nearly 10-15% died at sea throughout the so-called Middle Passage, not ever making their destination.

The fort then passed through the hands of the Dutch and even a local Fetu chief at some point, before being conquered by the British in 1664. Over the years the fort was increasingly used for the developing slave trade, which came to a peak in the 18th century. By 1700, the fort had been transformed into a castle and served as the headquarters of the British colonial governor.

Up to 1,000 male and 500 female slaves were shackled and crammed in the castle's dank, poorly ventilated dungeons, with no space to lie down and very little light. Without water or sanitation, the floor of the dungeon was littered with human waste and many captives fell seriously ill. The men were separated from the women, and the captors regularly raped the helpless women. The castle also featured confinement cells — small pitch-black spaces for prisoners who revolted or were rebellious. Once the slaves set foot in the castle, they could spend up to three months in captivity under these dreadful conditions before being shipped off to the New World.

In the Cape Coast Castle, the Smithsonian Institute helped set up a Museum of Slaves which now caters to an increasing number of African Americans - the descendants of slaves who arrive in search of their roots. Visitors weep as they come out of the dungeons at Cape Coast Castle, having seen where potentially their ancestors had been kept in the gloomy and damp, unlivable conditions before the Atlantic crossing to America or the Caribbean islands. The guides take them along a tunnel to what was known as 'the gate of no return'. A narrow slit in the castle wall, only wide enough for one at a time, opened onto the sea, the waiting ships, and yet another dehumanizing ordeal lie before them. Another revelation is the process by which the slaves were acquired, recent research by Dr Akosua Perbi of the

University of Ghana has shown a substantial African involvement in the trade. Typically, after an inter-tribal war, the prisoners taken by the winning side were sold to the castles.

It was a place where our ancestors were held as slaves and it was a powerful and moving experience when our group toured the area, very slowly, taking in the inhumanity that our ancestors endured in forced captivity where some died in the small, confined room from diseases and starvation and lack of basic needs for human decency and survival. This fort was a place where the ships came in originally for economic trading and became a place to take the Ghanaian people who survived as slaves to America and other ports foreign to the African natives.

When our missionary team left the slave fort there were inscriptions on one of the doors that read, "A Place of

No Return" and another was "We Are Sorry for What We Did to You." The statement asked forgiveness of those who had a part in capturing and selling the Ghanaian men and women into slavery.

We must remember God "created us in His image" not to treat people as enemies. The word of God says we ought to love one another as God has loved us. It is the enemy's (Satan's) job "to steal, kill and destroy." To murder or kill or end one another's life was never God's plan for the family of God or anyone else.

We as a people must know that God is about love, joy, and kindness. He gave us Jesus Christ as our role model, His Son. What He wants for this world is to be an example of His love. After our tour of the Cape Coast, we had lunch near the area. It was genuinely nice, as one of the local restaurants served us outside on the side of the Atlantic Ocean.

The Ghana Baptist Seminary School was also an institute that we were privileged to visit where our missionary group was introduced to the young Pastors.

Our women from the group were asked to sing songs and we were excited to sing praises to the Lord. As our voices filled the place everyone enjoyed the musical part of praise and worship.

The Ghana Baptist Seminary School

This school was going to be used for the young pastors in training for the week and some of the Pastors were recognized during the announcements.

The schedule was discussed about the classes that would take place the following days. Males of the gathering talked about their participation with sessions that would be happening. Because of their customs in Africa, our women's pastors were not able to attend the training classes at the Baptist Seminary School.

The Sunday Service

On Sunday, our missionary group visited a church in Accra, Africa. This church was founded in 1985, a white, two-story building and both levels were full of people, standing room only! There was a mixture of African people, some wore African attire while others wore

American clothing. The worship service was like the church services in America with a choir, scripture reading, and the Word of God. However, this church compared to the village church was much different.

The village church was a work in progress as they were just starting to build it. So far, the village church was only a frame with a top supported by poles, there were no walls.   However, I still remember the men and women shouting and dancing in worship.

There was a great difference in the spirit and level of enthusiasm in the white building town church from the village community church.

The Children's Hospital

When the missionary group visited the Children Hospital in Accra, West Africa, I felt empathy for these children because the medical equipment and supplies were substandard to meet their needs for proper medical care. And then someone from our missionary team asked me to pray. I thought quickly in my heart that this was an assignment from GOD and because of His great power it was easy to obey HIM.

As I prayed that day, I put those health and medical equipment problems in the hands of the Almighty God. I knew He had the power to strengthen their little hearts and to open doors to meet their needs. I knew that He was the one that could raise them off their beds of affliction.

I did what was asked of me that day with the confidence that God the Father had taken control of the situations for those children in that hospital on that day. We, too, must remember when we are going through sickness or disease, to put it in the hands of the Lord and leave it there.

The Lord has the power to heal all matters of disease and sickness. When we call on the name of the Lord Jesus Christ, He will fix it every time. We must remember a person's faith is what makes them whole.

My roommate and I discussed the poor babies in the "Children Hospital." The limitation of medical supplies and the need for proper sterilization. Thoughts were expressed by both of us as we put ourselves in the place of the mother and how we would feel if we were in their position. Only God knew how they really felt deep down in their hearts.

We had the opportunity to visit a Kente cloth factory where some went inside of the factory, and some stayed on the bus. I thought the factory was a place where material was sold, but later found that it was much more, it was a huge factory where the Kente cloth was made. In sharing the factory visit, my roommate talked with excitement in her voice and eyes. She said the factory was a huge place.

I could imagine what she was talking about because I had worked in a factory in America in Hillsborough, NC in the 1970's. When I was in the eleventh grade, I worked in the textile factory, The Cone Mills. One of my aunts started working there in 1972. She was a "spinner," keeping the yarn tied up so the machines would not run out prior to completely making the fabric. First, my aunt got my mother on as a worker. Mother worked there for a few years. Then, they got me hired on as a worker with the company I worked there for about a month and a half. At the textile factory, I also worked as a "spinner" making sure the yarn did not run out from the bobbin. If the yarn ran out, the "fixer" would have to come and restart the machine. The

Cone's Mill was where different kinds of material are made. They had numerous large weaving boards and yarns of material that were set side by side.

Similar ways of making material were done through factories in the USA. The Cone Mills in Hillsborough's factory was renamed in 2000 to The Historic Eno River Mill, which is located on Dimmock's Mill Road in Hillsborough, North Carolina.

The Historic Eno River Mill was renovated and changed from a textile mill to a multi-tenant business-related development. Now there are sixteen companies comprising the Cloth Mill at Eno River and The Expedition School, The Weaver Street Markets' commercial agencies, Mystery Brewing Company. Many Specialty manufacturers and distributors including pharmaceuticals, natural products and furniture are homes in the Mill. This River Mill maintains its era extended practice as a center for trade and industry action, supplying repurposed rooms for resourceful enterprises in a momentous locale. However, in nineteen seven-six I found out the textile job was not for me.

One day the local men came to visit and brought gifts for each of us that were Kente cloth. The material was cut like a necktie. We draped the material around our necks as our group sat and the Ghanaians talked with us about the history of the Kente cloth. Kente cloth (from ke prefix of

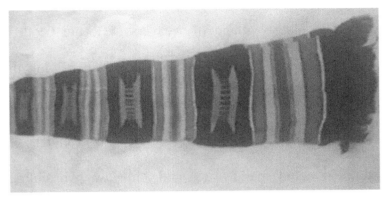

many Ashanti traditional area handwoven goods and nte –

from ntoma which means cloth) was created from the Ashanti people of Ghana. The Ashanti are a subgroup of the Akans people who have been around for over 600 years.

The oldest village of weavers of Kente Cloth is called Bonwire. The Bonwire weavers began making the cloth about 375 years ago. Bonwire is still the most famous center for Kente cloth weaving today. The legend is the traditional belief that Kurugu and Ameyaw, two siblings from the community, went hunting one evening and came across a spider spinning and rotating a web. The two brothers were astonished by the beauty of the web. They thought that they could create something like it. Upon returning home, they made the first cloth out of black and white fibers from a raffia tree. Traditional designs derived from one basic design called the Babadua. Generations of weavers modified their craft to create new patterns classified as Adwini. The colors woven in the Kente cloth have significant meanings. The blue thread symbolizes love, peace, harmony, and unity. Black strands represent maturity, mourning, and funerals. Gold and yellow colors exemplify signs of prosperity, comfort of circumstances, wealth, fertility, and the royal family. Red is a color of mourning death or funerals. Green represents spiritual growth: renewal and rebirth or vegetation: harvest, land, growth, and crops. Gray symbolizes healing, cleansing, traditions, and ceremonies. Purple is a sign of womanhood and ladylikeness. Silver is the color of joy, peace, moon, and romance. The white color in the Kente cloth is purity, cleansing traditions and festivals celebrations.

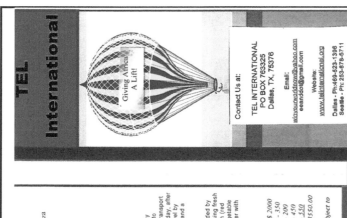

TEL International

Giving Africa A Lift!

Contact Us at:

TEL INTERNATIONAL
PO BOX 763325
Dallas, TX, 75376

Email:
wlovourworldnow@yahoo.com
eeanddot@gmail.com

Website:
www.telinternational.org

Dallas - Ph:469-523-1396
Seattle - Ph: 253-878-5711

Nkoranza

Teams fly into the capital city, Accra, stay overnight, and fly north the next morning to Kumasi or Sunyani. A van will meet and transport them to the Nkoranza Guesthouse. Each day, after an American style breakfast, they will travel by van to their ministry areas. Bottled water and a pack lunch will be provided.

The evening meals are planned and provided by Sister Taylor and the guesthouse staff, using fresh chicken (Tyson's). Can meats or fresh fish (red snapper) with rice, cabbage, or mixed vegetable dishes. There is hot and cold running water with tiled bathrooms, and clean linen.

Estimated cost of the Trip

Flight to Ghana	approx. - $ 2000
Flight North	350
Translators /Helpers	200
Transport/Luggage	450
Rooms/Food /Laundry	50
Total	**3550.00**

Prices based on 2010 costs and are subject to adjustment if prices vary.

Sponsorship Programs

Feed a family each month	$50
Help support and train a pastor	$60
Drill and complete a water well	$15,000
Build a 4- room school Block	$15,000
Build a full 8-room school	$25,000
Send a child to school Monthly	$25
Send a bale of children's clothing	$200
Send a bale of Adult clothing	$250
Build a 30x 50 foot Church	$28,000
Help the Taylor's Travel to Africa	$25

A Typical schedule for a team in Africa:

6:30 - 7:30 am —Personal Care & Prayer
7:30-8:45 am –Breakfast & Group Devotions
9am – 4:00pm ————— Ministry Outreach
4:00 – 5:30————————— Free Time
5:30pm——————— Group Dinner/Reports
7:30pm——————— Evening Activity or Rest
10:30 pm————— Devotions &Lights Out!

Ministry Supplies:

All teams must bring ministry supplies, such as books, lessons, workbooks, games, crafts and medicines, whether for children's camps, medical team or evangelism outreach. We recommend each person bring one suitcase for themselves and one filled with supplies for the ministry. Teams are also asked to help with one of the above areas of need for one of the local villages.

Dress: The weather is mild to hot, requiring only light weight wash and wear cotton mixtures. The local staff washes the laundry by hand. T-shirts and blouses with skirts should be taken by the women and jeans, Khaki trousers, and cotton shirts worn by the men. Dress suits are not required.

87

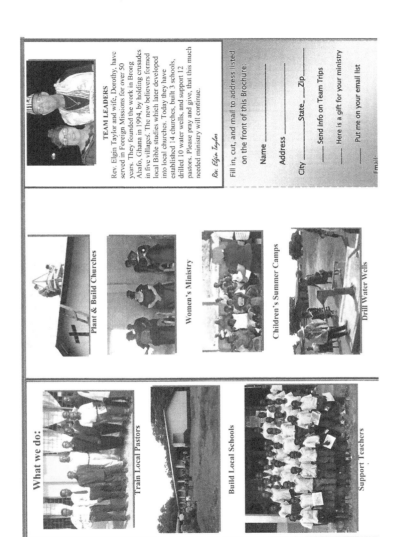

TEAM LEADERS

Rev. Elgin Taylor and wife, Dorothy, have served in Foreign Missions for over 50 years. They founded the work in Brong Ahafo, Ghana in 1994, by holding crusades in five villages. The new believers formed local Bible studies which later developed into local churches. Today they have established 14 churches, built 3 schools, drilled 10 water wells, and support 12 pastors. Please pray and give, that this much needed ministry will continue.

Rev. Elgin Taylor

Fill in, cut, and mail to address listed on the front of this Brochure.

Name _____

Address _____

City _____ State ____ Zip ____

_____ Send info on Team Trips

_____ Here is a gift for your ministry

_____ Put me on your email list

Email:

What we do:

Train Local Pastors

Plant & Build Churches

Women's Ministry

Children's Summer Camps

Drill Water Wells

Build Local Schools

Support Teachers

Chapter Five

Tel-International

Tel International Missions Society is focused on sustaining the work of foreign nationals that reach out with the love of Jesus Christ by sharing the gospel and compassionately meeting the needs of hurting people, evangelizing the lost, discipling the saved and establishing new converts into the body and ministry of local Christian churches.

Tel's core values are to be:

Evangelism Focused: The Great Commission compels us to make evangelism our primary focus. We plan to initiate, coordinate, facilitate and oversee missions and outreach programs that invite, welcome, encourage and inspire persons to join in and experience the gospel of Jesus Christ and the new life He offers. Everything we do must filter through the desire for and the purpose of evangelizing the world. Christ commanded it. We must do it.

Discipleship Driven: Matthew 28:19 clearly demonstrates that evangelism is incomplete without making disciples. Disciples do more than merely believe; they obey the Lord, adhering to His ways. To make a disciple requires teaching, mentoring, and modeling the lifestyle of Jesus. Discipleship involves growth towards maturity and teaching converts to become "disciples". The work of discipleship is the work of multiplication, not addition, meaning it starts slow and builds over time. Jesus had thousands of people come to hear him preach. But the primary discipleship work took place not even in his small group of the twelve, but in Peter,

James and John who were with him at key points in his life, learned by experiencing how Jesus handled things, and became the leaders who could carry on once Jesus left. We will be patient enough to do the slow groundwork initially to have a powerful impact over the long-term.

Church Centered: We are committed to being a Mission that begins, nurtures, and equips churches to be the expression of Christ in their communities and to reach out with indigenous or native missionary vision and action.

Compassion Motivated: Compassion is a common virtue that moves us to reach out to the whole man. We care deeply about the dignity of people who suffer in our world and are motivated by God's love to bring love, hope and peace to people in need. We enjoy interacting with nationals and feel a deep satisfaction in our friendships with them. As we labor alongside them, we become emboldened by what we see as opportunities present themselves.

Integrity Guided: We are honest in our communications, transparent and accountable in our finances and trustworthy in our relationships. We conduct ourselves and our missionary society in ways which are highly ethical and above reproach.

Currently, the coordinator for Ghana is Julius Nuongtah Nangai.

Tel-International was founded by Reverend Elgin and Dorothy Taylor in 1994. They worked diligently for centuries in Africa. The school and organization have been placed in the hands of the administrators of Ghana.

Newsletter 1999

In the November 1999 newsletter, Christians in Action, Missions Update, Reverend Elgin Taylor, International

Director, commented on the trip to Ghana, West Africa. He stated that when we arrived in Kumasi that our missionary group was to turn a switch in our minds stating, "This is Africa, not America, and things are done differently here. Remember, not wrong, but different."

Some of the experiences mentioned in his newsletter talked about the Ashanti Region and the Ghana Leadership Conference, visiting the Ghanaian Baptist Seminary upon arrival for devotional service the first day the Leadership Conference was full of African clergy. Many African pastors had traveled by bus, bicycle, and foot for hours. These clergymen praised God and danced Ghanaian style that day. These pastors were overjoyed to be there and to be able to take part in service.

Because of the partnership with New Canaan Baptist (NC), Glenarden First Baptist (MD), The L.A. Centinela

Foundation (CA) and many other churches and individuals, the CinA were able to provide strategic training for one hundred and twenty pastors that registered. Reverend Taylor gave thanks to all who made the Conference possible. He also thanked the clergy in attendance who shared their faith in teaching the ministry, e.g., Pastors Jenkins, Farrar, and Goerz. Reverend Taylor gave special thanks to Missionaries Attawia and Kargbo for sharing experiences from Sierra Leone.

The newsletter mentioned a few of the seminar topics: Pastors Servanthood, Effective Pastoring, Shepherding and Serving, Marriage, Family & Polygamy, Pressure of Church Planning, Handling the Financial, Learning to Send Faxes and E-mails, and God During Political Upheavals. Ephesians: 4 was the Conference Theme: "Unity in the Spirit," during this great session.

One pastor who had no Bible spoke with a tribal dialect from Upper Volta. This preacher interpreted the New Testament working with a missionary who had come back to Africa. His means of transportation to attend the seminar was walking through thick brush. To complete the translation of the Bible into the language of his people, it was urgent to journey to the conference. Another pastor traveled by bicycle and walked long distances to attend the classes. This was an inspiration to everyone, and the pastor was overjoyed with God's glory.

He was from a poverty-stricken village and poorly dressed. There was a joyful expression all over him. He blessed the entire gathering with his enthusiasm in worship and praise. He was a gifted song leader and divine warrior which was illustrated in his final prayer. This culture of people is wonderful individuals that may not have material things or money.

Several team members asked questions after meeting such dedicated servants of God. The team members asked: "What is the real meaning of being poor and poverty stricken?" One answer was: Many people have wealth and material things but are unfortunately unhappy not having Christ in their lives.

Included in Reverend Taylor's newsletter was other missionary trips that took place that year. One team was from New Cannan trip to Porto Alegre; Brazil and the other team was from Glenarden First Baptist going to Colombia, South America.

He wrote in his newsletter about the success of all the trips on the various missionary journeys. Nine team members were on the trip to Brazil, besides the nine who went to Ghana. He wrote that the group was on fire for the Lord and were blessed to have a pastor who loved missions.

This team was accommodated by the Spencers and Powers at the Christians in Action Ranch not far from Porto Alegre, Brazil. The team from Glenarden First Baptist embarked to Cartagena, Colombia. A pilot program from their church managed by CinA East Coast Representatives. Cartagena and the Afro-heritage village of Palenque the team had a productive outreach. The last week of the trip the outreach was on a neighboring island. Which consisted of two days roughing it among the chickens, goats, and pigs, in a small village, but they were satisfied with souls for Christ.

Chapter Six

The Journey Home

Before leaving Ghana there were some things that were particularly important about the trip. In the region of Ghana, we met some nice people. People that were friendly. Those that were caring, sharing, loving and sincere of their heart from God.

Fellowship among these individuals was precious. Being away from family and friends and traveling to a foreign land, could have been awfully hard to endure. However, meeting Ghanaians who had a genuine heart for others and exemplified love for people from a totally different background magnified the beauty of this journey and awesomeness of our God. Retracing our steps back through Kumasi and Accra, we gathered back at the couple house.

During our forty-minute reprieve, we enjoyed nibbling on sandwiches and resting before our flight back to the United States. This was the same couple's house that we visited the first morning that we arrived in Ghana, and they showed the same hospitality and courtesy as when we first met them. This time we had the pleasure of meeting their son who was about nine or ten years old. He was a very polite child. He talked with us and carried on conversations about his experience in Ghana and school. I went to the bathroom while at the house and was shocked to find a baby lizard. After telling their son about the baby lizard, he came and got the animal telling me not to be fearful that it was harmless. After listening to him my thoughts were, I did not want to touch the creature.

Ghana: West Africa Mission (1999)

Leaving Accra and Kumasi, Ghana, West Africa was an incredibly quiet experience. No one on the bus in our Missionary Group spoke, I can only imagine that they were reflecting on all that we had seen, heard, and learned. We had come to Ghana, West Africa on a Mission that God had impressed on the heart of Pastor Farrar and then birthed the passion in the hearts of the missionary group to come alongside him to see the manifestation. On this mission assignment, we experienced love, joy and peace that exceeded our expectations. Relationships were formed within our group and with those that we encountered and fellowshipped with. The trip back involved our group flight leaving out of Accra, Ghana on August twenty-five nineteen ninety-nine. It was a sunny day and a smooth ride. Our flight from Ghana to London lasted about six hours. Once we reached London, we traveled via the

London/Gatwick British Airways to Charlotte, NC. From Charlotte, we made our way to Raleigh. Our plane landed in Raleigh/Durham Airport on August twenty-six nineteen-nine at about 6:00 p.m. Even with all the connecting flights, I experienced no anxiety on the flight home, a far cry from the ride to Accra. Though I was met with a challenge when my husband and I left the airport.

When arriving home, the moment we pulled up in the yard under the carport I could see that something had happened. I asked my husband about the carport; the damage was quite noticeable in that something had hit the railing over the driveway. And it was knocked to the edge of the brick and that part of the roof was not sitting right. My husband said he had not noticed it. I told him the railing on the side was shifted more to the right side. His response was he did not know, and he had not even seen the damage to the carport.

As we got out of the vehicle and entered the house I spoke and hugged the children and immediately asked them about the damage to the side of the carport. Their eyes got big as a fifty-cent piece, and they would not respond to my question! I was fierce, I told them I wanted to know what happened and wanted to know right then but their lips were sealed. It took about two days before someone told me what happened.

I had already talked to the neighbor across the street about fixing the carport. After discussing the problem with him, immediately he came over and checked out the carport and he told me it had been hit with a car. He came over and used a jack and got back it to the spot it was supposed to be. I thanked him and asked him how much he charged, he was so nice and did not charge me anything.

Now that was a good neighbor, he also had two daughters, and he knew what it was like being a parent.

As I think about it, we were the first group of missionaries from our church to go to Africa. I thanked God! The Lord not only took care of our missionary team to Africa and back, but He also took care of our families too.

I know after this trip there were many blessed people from the group who had received abundantly from the Lord. Mother was doing okay and was still at her home in Haw River, NC. That was a joy to behold. My roommate later would have her house remodeled after the water damage, she had discussed with me in Accra, West Africa.

One of the pastors from our trip was blessed. His ministry grew and now he has a multitude of members. His church is on a campus and surely, he is pleased with how the Lord has used him. And I know of several other blessings the team has received, it is allowed to God, to Him belongs all the Honor & the Glory. Knowing if we take care of His work, He will take care of us. It is all in the name of Christ that we do what we do, so that He will get the Glory. Hallelujah! Amen!

Reflections on my Family History

To think this was a culture that our ancestors had been forcefully separated from more than two thousand years ago. It is such a travesty of justice and human dignity to have been forcefully removed from what you know and love.

My father's great-great Aunt rode on a slave ship from Africa to a land that was completely foreign to her. Our native homeland that the Lord had opened a door for this group of Missionaries to come and share the life and the light of Christ Jesus. The trip lasted about nineteen days with us being blessed and privileged to interact with different cultures and ethnicities.

My grandfather, Papa, was born in the 1900's. My grandparents had the same last name before they were married. My oldest daughter discovered this while doing research on our family history. This fact was confirmed when I talked to my aunt in 2020. It was customary during slavery, that when our ancestors were sold, they would assume the name of their slave owners as their last name.

The Prey family lived in the same neighborhood as the Foust family. It was interesting to hear that when they would visit the Prey family, they were acknowledged as cousins.

Missionary Team Comments

"As I taught the seminar and saw the hunger to learn on the pastor's faces, I would describe them as very receptive and open. It was exciting to share some of my pastoral experiences with them."

-Pastor John Jenkins, Glenarden First Baptist, Maryland

"Awesome! Overwhelming: That's what comes to me after going into Kumasi and seeing people everywhere on the streets selling things. Those African women seemed so content, even with huge loads on their backs." -

Jacqueline, NC

"My impressions were of the strong hearts of the people. Everyone, even the children, is busy selling something. They keep busy just about every day, no weekend off like us." -Belinda, NC

"It was a life changing experience for me. I never thought I would visit Africa, let alone be there helping in the villages. We are already planning another trip next year and take more clothing and goods to the northern region. The people's joy in worshipping God in spite of their circumstances was a delight to hold!" - LA. Johnson, VA

'My lasting impression was of how industrious, patient, and humble the people were with so little. How does one compare or describe their strength for survival through great oppression and poverty?

God's will for my life became clearer while there, to return as a missionary nurse."

-Ruth, NC

"I didn't feel like a stranger or a foreigner at all, in fact, I felt at home. It was like seeing myself in the faces of all those peoples as they worshiped God in His glory, majesty, and splendor! Praise Him for loving me so much as to take me to a higher level of ministry in Him." - Karona, NC

"My expectation of Africa was distorted by the media images I had seen. I expected to see many undernourished and sickly children, who had nothing at all but mud huts. It was nice to see that conditions were better than expected but still needy. The idea of my being a long-lost sister snatched from this continent was so refreshing."

- Gertrude

This book is not only in the memory of the Late Bishop *Leonard "Foday" Farrar, but also the Late Reverend Elgin Taylor.*

A Tribute:

The Late Reverend Elgin Earl Taylor went to be with the Lord in August 2021. He was a true servant of God who will be greatly missed.

References

1. Aki, Evi. Flavors of Africa: Discover Authentic Family Recipes from All over the Continent. Page Street Publishing 2019.

2. Lilian Diarra, "Ghana's Slave Castles: The Shocking Story of the Ghanaian Cape Coast," Culture Trip, accessed March 12, 2022, https://theculturetrip.com/africa/ghana/articles/ ghana-s-slave-castles-the-shocking-story-of-the-ghanaian-cape coast/?amp=1.

3. "Kente cloth inspired by a spiders web," The African Gourmet, accessed March 12. 2022, https://www.theafricangourmet.com/2019/05/african-kente -cloth-facts.html?m=1.

4. Evi Aki: 'Grilled Tilapia with Ginger Pepper, Yassa

(Senegalese Lemon Chicken), Fufu, Banku and Jollof Rice'
Flavors of Africa (2018)

5. "Cape Coast Castle Museum," Museum of African Modern
Art, accessed March 12, 2022,
https://momaa.org/directory/cape-coast-
castle-museum.

6. "Ghana's Geography," Ghana Web, accessed March 12,
2022, www.ghanaweb.com/GhanaHomePage/geography/
kumasi.php.

7. "Former Liberian president Charles Taylor found guilty of
war crimes," History, accessed March 12, 2022,
https.//www.history.com/this-day-in-history/former-liberian-pre
sident-charles-taylor-found-guilty-of-war-crimes.

8. "Kente Cloth Colors," Kente Cloth, accessed March 12,

2022, https: www.kentecloth.net/kente-cloth-colors.

9. Telinternational.org. Accessed 13 May 2020.

10. Fage, J. D. , Boateng, . Ernest Amano , Maier, . Donna J. and Davies, . Oliver (2021, September 30). Ghana Map [Digital image]. Retrieved from Britannica.com/place/Ghana.

About The Author

Minister Belinda McBroom is a licensed minister, missionary and author of the book *"West Africa Missions in Ghana (1999)" A Personal Experience*.

Her missionary work and her never ending faith in God led to writing her book describing a trip to Ghana, West Africa in 1999. She found the trip to be a glorious personal experience which also served to further strengthen her faith in God.

An important purpose of her mission to Ghana, was to learn more about its people, their cultures and traditions in hope that she will be able to help clear up current and past misconceptions about this African country.

A portion of your purchase of this book will be donated to Tel International. To be a blessing to the author, please email belindaandGod@yahoo.com or visit: www.belindamcbroom.com for more information.

Ghana: West Africa Mission (1999)

Made in the USA
Columbia, SC
24 August 2022

65030333R10065